SCHIRMER'S LIBRARY
OF MUSICAL CLASSICS

FERDINAND SIEBER

Thirty-Six
Eight-Measure Vocalises

For Elementary Vocal Teaching

IN SIX EDITIONS

G. SCHIRMER, *Inc.*

DISTRIBUTED BY

HAL•LEONARD®
CORPORATION

7777 W. BLUEMOUND RD. P.O. BOX 13819 MILWAUKEE, WI 53213

Printed in the U. S. A.

Elementary Vocalises
for
Baritone.

FERD. SIEBER. Op.96.

N. B. All the exercises are to be sung, at first, on various vowels (a, o, e), and, later, on the syllables written under them. Do *not* observe, at first, the directions given for shading, but execute each exercise in a quiet, smooth *piano,* and as *legato* as possible. The tempo to be employed depends on the needs and the ability of the singer. At every rest, and at the breathing-marks(✛), breath *must* be taken; it *may* also be taken (if necessary) at the commas(ꝱ).

Printed in the U. S. A.

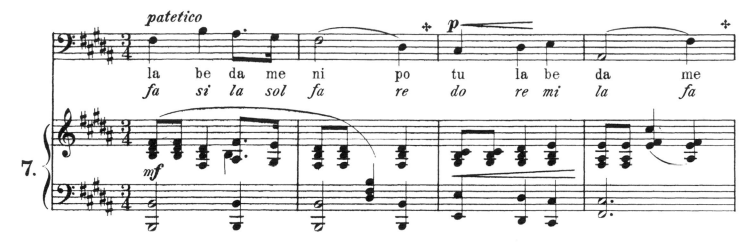

21.

la be_ da me___ ni___ po | tu la be da me ____ ni
do la_ do mi_ fa___ fa | *do do fa sol_ la ___ la*

po _____ tu _____ la ___ be | da ___ me ____ ni
re _____ la ___ fa ___ fa | *do _____ sol ___ fa*

col canto

22.

da me ni_ po ___ | tu la be da ____
re la sol_ re | *si mi re do*

mf

me ni po tu ___ | la___ be ___ da ___ me
sol si sol fa ___ | *re ___ si_ la ___ re*

col canto

33.

34.

SCHIRMER'S LIBRARY
of Musical Classics

SONG COLLECTIONS

The Library Volume Number is given in brackets: [1363]

ALBUM OF SACRED SONGS. A Collection of 22 Favorite Songs suitable for use in the churches.
High [1384]; Low [1385]

ANTHOLOGY OF ITALIAN SONG OF THE 17TH AND 18TH CENTURIES. 59 Songs. i. e.
Book I [290]; Book II [291]

BEETHOVEN, L. VAN
AN DIE FERNE GELIEBTE (To the Distant Beloved) A cycle of 6 songs. Op. 98. g. e. High [616]; Low [617]
SIX SONGS. g. e. High [618]; Low [619]

BRAHMS, J.
FIFTY SELECTED SONGS. g. e. Low [1581]; High [1582]

CHOPIN, F.
SEVENTEEN POLISH SONGS. Op. 74. g. e. High [249]; Low [250]

FIELITZ, A. VON
ELILAND. A cycle of 10 songs. Op. 9. g. e. Medium [694]; High [695]

FOSTER, S. C.
ALBUM OF SONGS. 20 Favorite Compositions. Collected and edited by H. V. Milligan [1439]

FRANZ, R.
VOCAL ALBUM. 62 Songs. g. e. High [1572]; Low [1573]

GRIEG, E.
SELECTED SONGS. g. e. High [1592]; Low [1593]

LISZT, F.
TWELVE SONGS. g. or f. & e. Low [1613]; High [1614]

MENDELSSOHN, F.
SIXTEEN SELECTED SONGS. g. e. Low [1644]; High [1645]
SIXTEEN TWO-PART SONGS. g. e. [377]

SCHUBERT, F.
FIRST VOCAL ALBUM (3 Cycles, and 24 Favorite Songs). g. e. High [342]; Low [343]
THE MAID OF THE MILL (Die schöne Müllerin) A cycle of 20 songs. g. e. High [344]; Low [345]
WINTER-JOURNEY (Die Winterreise) A cycle of 24 songs. g. e. High [346]; Low [347]
TWENTY-FOUR FAVORITE SONGS. g. e. High [350]; Low [351]
SECOND VOCAL ALBUM. 82 Songs. g. e. [352]

SCHUMANN, R.
VOCAL ALBUM. 55 Songs. g. e. High [120]; Low [121]
WOMAN'S LIFE AND LOVE (Frauenliebe und -leben) A cycle of 8 songs. g. e. High [1356]; Low [1357]

TCHAIKOVSKY, P. I.
TWELVE SONGS. g. e. Low [1620]; High [1621]

WAGNER, R.
FIVE SONGS. g. e. Low [1181]; High [1233]

(Languages of texts are shown in small letters: e. = English; f. = French; g. = German;
i. = Italian. Where there is no other indication, texts are in English only.)
Any Schirmer Library volume may be obtained in cloth binding. Prices will be quoted on request.

G. SCHIRMER, *Inc.* New York

A-1805